Science That's Appropriate <u>and</u> Doable

This science resource book was written with two goals in mind:

- to provide "good" science for your students
- to make it easy for you

What makes this book "good" science?

When you follow the step-by-step lessons in this book, you'll be using an instructional model that makes science education relevant to real life.

- Your students will be drawn in by interesting activities that encourage them to express what they already know about a concept.

- Your students will participate in hands-on discovery experiences and be guided to describe the experiences in their own words. Together, you'll record the experiences in both class and individual logbooks.

- You'll provide explanations and vocabulary that will help your students accurately explain what they have experienced.

- Your students will have opportunities to apply their new understandings to new situations.

What makes this book easy for you?

- The step-by-step activities are easy to understand and have illustrations where it's important.

- The resources you need are at your fingertips — record sheets; logbook forms; and other reproducibles such as minibooks, task cards, picture cards, and pages to make into overhead transparencies.

- Each science concept is presented in a self-contained section. You can decide to do the entire book or pick only those sections that enhance your own curriculum.

> For sites on the World Wide Web that supplement the material in this resource book, go to http://www.evan-moor.com and look for the <u>Product Updates</u> link on the main page.

Using Logbooks as Learning Tools

Logbooks are valuable learning tools for several reasons:
- Logbooks give students an opportunity to put what they are learning into their own words.
- Putting ideas into words is an important step in internalizing new information. Whether spoken or written, this experience allows students to synthesize their thinking.
- Explaining and describing experiences help students make connections between several concepts and ideas.
- Logbook entries allow the teacher to catch misunderstandings right away and then reteach.
- Logbooks are a useful reference for students and a record of what has been learned.

Two Types of Logbooks

The Class Logbook

A class logbook is completed by the teacher and the class together. The teacher records student experiences and helps students make sense of their observations. The class logbook is a working document. You will return to it often for a review of what has been learned. As new information is acquired, make additions and corrections to the logbook.

Individual Science Logbooks

Individual students process their own understanding of investigations by writing their own responses in their own logbooks. Two types of logbook pages are provided in this unit.

1. Open-ended logbook pages:
   Pages 4 and 5 provide two choices of pages that can be used to respond to activities in the unit. At times you may wish students to write in their own logbooks and then share their ideas as the class logbook entry is made. After the class logbook has been completed, allow students to revise and add information to their own logbooks. At other times you may wish students to copy the class logbook entry into their own logbooks.

2. Specific logbook pages:
   You will find record forms or activity sheets following many activities that can be added to each student's logbook.

At the conclusion of the unit, reproduce a copy of the logbook cover on page 3 for each student. Students can then organize both types of pages and staple them with the cover.

_____'s
Simple Machines
Logbook

Simple Machines • EMC 860

Name _____

This is what I learned about Simple Machines today:

Note: Reproduce this form for students to record science investigations for their individual logbooks.

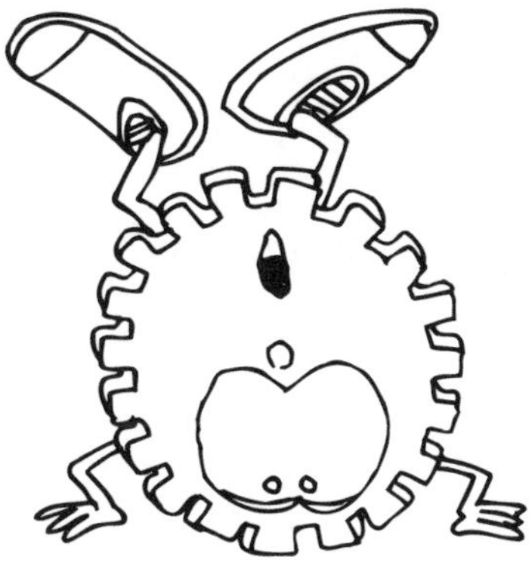

Name ______________________________

Investigation: ______________________________

What we did:

____

____

____

What we saw:

____

____

____

What we learned:

____

____

____

Work is done when a force is used to move something over a distance.

Who Is Working?

- Form teams of "observers" to report work that is being done. Set a time limit and assign a recorder. (This could be a parent helper or a cross-age tutor.)

  One team should watch the class.
  One team should tour the school.
  One team should observe students and staff during a recess time.
  One team should observe the school's neighbors.

  When the observations are completed have each team describe the work that they saw.

- Begin your Simple Machines class logbook with a page entitled "Who Is Working?" List the work observed on the chart.

Who Is Working?

Emily is reading.

Pam is sharpening her pencil.

Joe is eating.

What Is Work?

Reproduce the individual logbook form on page 11. In the final section of the page, students write a definition of work in their own words.

> At this point, the definitions that students write may not be completely accurate. The important thing is that they have thoughtfully expressed themselves. You will provide new experiences that will allow students to develop accurate concepts. (A definition of work is given on page 8.)

Work Relays

• Choose teams and play several relay games.

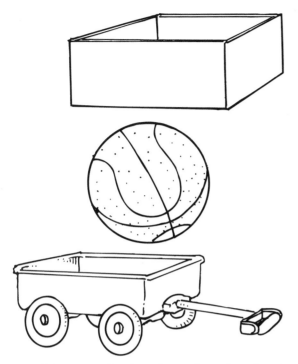

Relay 1
Each member of a team will push a large box across the floor to another member of the team, who lifts the box and carries it back to the original starting line. Repeat this push and lift until all team members have had a turn.

Relay 2
Each member of the team will dribble a ball to another team member who picks up the ball and carries it back to the original starting line. Repeat this dribble and carry until all have had a turn.

Relay 3
Use a wagon. Each member of the team will pull the empty wagon to another team member, who then takes over and takes the wagon back to the original starting line. Repeat this pull until all team members have had a turn.

• Discuss whether the relays involved any work. Record all student responses on a page of the class logbook entitled "Work Relays." You will refer back to the logbook to evaluate the responses in Looking Back on page 9.

Try asking the following questions:

"Was any part of the relay work?"
(Student responses will vary. Some may respond that it was work because they had to run fast, the box was big, or that they carried something to a new place. You are hoping for responses that indicate moving something over a distance.)

"What made it work?"
(Again responses will vary. "It made me sweat. I was out of breath when I finished. I moved the wagon to the other end.")

"Is the relay like any other work that you have seen?"
(Students might note that construction workers carry bricks or boards from one location to another. The building manager at your school may push boxes of paper and other supplies on a cart from the office to a storage room.)

Work Relays

Push and Lift Box

It was work because we had to carry it.

It was big.

A carpenter carries boards from one place to another.

       Simple Machines • EMC 860

Classroom Jobs

- Assign a classroom job to a group of students. Make sure that the jobs are things that need to be done in your classroom so that the activity is "real." Students might:

> organize a bookshelf
> water the plants
> sharpen the pencils in the
>   pencil bank
>
> straighten a center
> count the playground balls
> clean out desks

- Before reproducing page 12 for individual students, fill in the names of four of the jobs.

- Take time to talk about what was done in each job and whether it was work. Record the jobs and observations on a new class logbook page entitled "Classroom Jobs." Compare these ideas with those generated following the relays.

A Push Is a Force

- Ask your school custodian to come to your classroom with his cart. Have a student stand on the cart as the custodian pushes it across the room. Ask students to speculate about whether or not pushing was work and why.

- Record the students' ideas on a class logbook page entitled "What Is Work?"

- After the students have given their ideas, help students explain work more precisely. You might say something like:

"When Mr. Ruiz pushed Jon across the room he was doing work. Scientists call the push Mr. Ruiz gave the cart a **force**. When a person applies a force to a cart it moves over a distance. In science we say that **we do work when we use a force to move something over a distance**. If the object does not move, it is not considered work."

- Write the definition of work on the class logbook page.

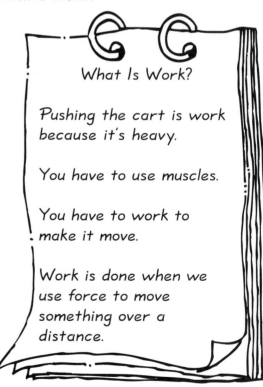

What Is Work?

Pushing the cart is work because it's heavy.

You have to use muscles.

You have to work to make it move.

Work is done when we use force to move something over a distance.

Check for Understanding

Reproduce the task cards on page 13 and cut them out. Put the
cards in a basket. Students draw a card from a basket and
actually do or pretend to do the task.

Then the class decides whether work, according to the scientific
definition, was done. After each task, ask:
"Was there a force? What?"
"Did something move? What?"
"Was work done?" (There must be force and movement for scientists to call it work.)

Answer Key for Tasks

Task	Force	What Moved	Was Work Done?
1	the push	the chair	Yes
2	the push	nothing	No
3	lifting	the crayon	Yes
4	walking	the student	Yes
5	kicking	the ball	Yes
6	none	nothing	No
7	hand pushing	chalk	Yes
8	none	nothing	No
9	hand and arm turning	the pages	Yes
10	fingers pushing	the keys	Yes
11	none	nothing	No
12	no force from rider	the car moves	The rider does not work; the car works.

Looking Back

Take time to look back at your class
logbook. Have students decide which
of the recorded observations scientists
would have called work. Ask students to
identify the force and movement in each
case. Highlight these tasks.

Force -
lifting and walking
Movement -
carrying can to plants

Classroom Jobs
I moved the books to the
right places and stood
them up.

I pointed at each ball and
said a number.

I filled the watering can,
carried it to the plants,
and poured the water.

Force -
lifting
Movement -
move books

Force-
pointing finger
Movement -
none

Work At Home

Reproduce the logbook page on page 14. Students will complete the form at home and record work that they see being done.

When they bring the pages back, share the ideas. Check to make sure that students identify the force and movement in each example.

A Book of Work

Reproduce page 15 for each student and make an overhead transparency of the page. Complete the transparency to use as a model.

Brainstorm and list work that is done in your classroom and around the school.

Give each student a copy of page 15 and share the model you have made.

Have each student draw and write about one example of work from the list. Share the pages and then bind them into a class book.

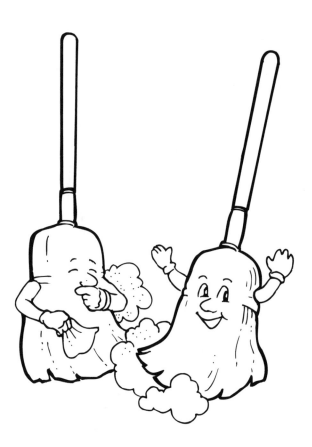

Name _____

What Is Work?

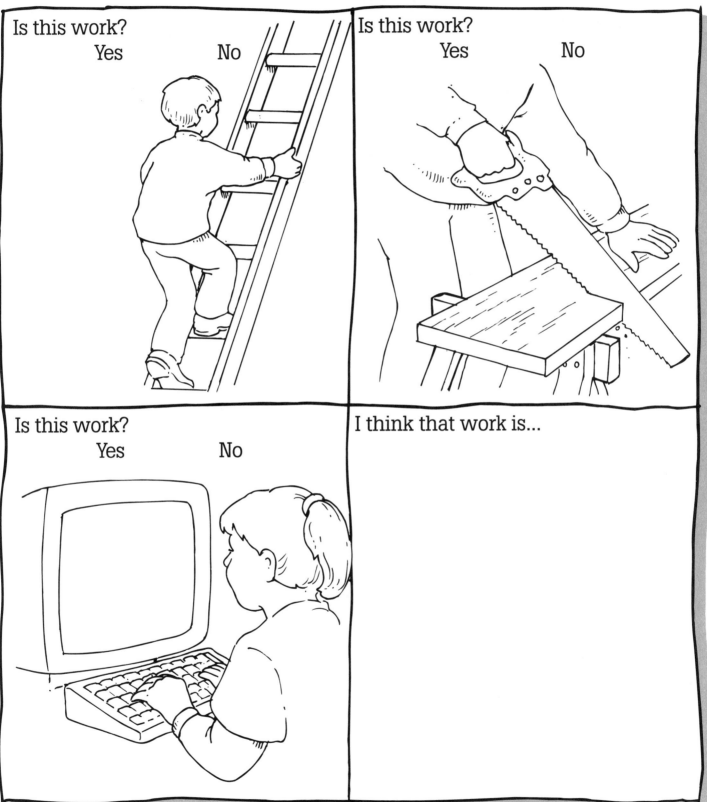

Is this work?
Yes   No

Is this work?
Yes   No

Is this work?
Yes   No

I think that work is...

Simple Machines • EMC 860

Note: Reproduce this form for each student to use with page 8.

Name _____

Jobs in Our Classroom

Job	What does this person do?	Is it work?	Have I done it?

Simple Machines • EMC 860

1

Push a roller chair
across the room.

  2

Push against the
chalkboard with your hand.

  3

Take a crayon out of the
crayon tub.

 4

Walk to the door.

  5

Kick a ball.

 6

Don't move. Sit where you are.

  7

Write a number on the chalkboard.

 8

Read the words on the
bulletin board.

  9

Turn the pages and read a book.

 10

Write your name using a computer.

  11

Watch a video.

 12

Ride in a car.

Note: Reproduce this form for each student to use with page 10.

Name _____

Work at My House

This is work.   This is not work.

Force = _____

Motion = _____

This is work.   This is not work.

Force = _____

Motion = _____

This is work.   This is not work.

Force = _____

Motion = _____

I saw this work at my house:

Force = _____

Motion = _____

       Simple Machines • EMC 860

Name _____

Work at School

Job:

Force:

Movement:

Draw the work.

Some jobs take more work than other jobs.

How Much Work Is It?

Use this activity to get students thinking about the amount of work a job involves.

- Ask a student to lift a book from the floor and put it on a shelf. Students should recognize that work is done. (The force is the lift; the book moved to the shelf.)

  Have a second student lift an identical book and place it on the same shelf. Ask, "Did (student 2) do the same amount of work as (student 1)?"

- Record student responses on a page in the class logbook entitled "How Much Work?"

  You are listening for the idea that the work was the same because it took the same amount of force to move the book the same distance.

     Do not expect students to use exact vocabulary at this point.
     Do not give them the answer.
     Do ask questions that may lead them to correct conclusions.
        "Are the two books the same size?"
        "Which shelf did _____ use?
        "What about _____?"
        "Was it harder to lift one book than the other?"

- Ask students to suggest ways to make the job more work. Record the suggestions on the class logbook page.

Is It More Work?

- Use the same bookshelf and two identical books. Have a student move one book from the floor to the lowest shelf and then move the second book to the highest shelf.

  Ask questions to help students to synthesize the information that they have observed.
  "Did _____ do any work?"
  "Were the books the same size?"
  "Were the shelves the same height?"
  "Did the books move the same distance?"
  "Do you think _____ did the same amount of work to move each book?"
  "Which book required more work?"

> The force required to move the book to the higher shelf was greater. Although the books were the same, the distance was different. Greater distances require more force.

- Change the situation. Have one student simultaneously put two books of the same size on the highest shelf and another student put one book of the same size on the same shelf. Ask:
  "Did one 'shelver' do more work than the other?"
  "Were the books the same size?"
  "Was the distance the same?"
  "What was different?"
  "Did that make the force required different?"

> The force required to move two books was greater. Although the distance was the same, the number of books (and therefore the weight) was different. More weight requires more force.

- Record responses on the "How Much Work?" class logbook page.

  You are looking for statements that contain these ideas: *"Jimmy did more work when he moved the book to the top shelf because he moved it farther. Lee did more work than Jessica because his books weighed more."*

         Simple Machines • EMC 860

Changing the Job to Make It More Work

- Refer to the "work" previously highlighted in the class logbook and "The Work at Home" page that was completed earlier. Brainstorm and list other work that children or families might do.

- Divide the class into groups of two or three. Have each group act out some work being done.

  After each group has shown their work, talk about the force and the movement involved. Challenge the class to tell how the same job might require more work.

  Have them describe how the force or the movement changed to require more work.

- Help students to reach the following generalizations and record them on the "How Much Work?" logbook page.

> - more work is required when a greater force is needed
> - more work is required when the distance moved is greater

How Much Work?

- *pushing a grocery cart loaded with groceries*

- *the grocery cart might have more items in it*

- *digging a hole in the garden*

- *the hole might need to be two feet deeper*

- *emptying the trash*

- *there might be rocks in the trash cans instead of paper*

Check For Understanding

Reproduce the individual logbook page on page 19. Have students complete the activity sheet showing a job and how to change the job to require more work and less work.

Share the answers as a class. Discuss and correct any misconceptions. Reinforce the generalization that the amount of work being done depends on the amount of force used and/or the distance moved.

Use New Understandings

Observe workers in the school doing jobs. Have students explain in their own words what would make each job easier or harder.

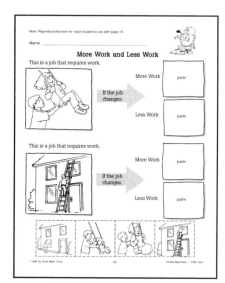

Simple Machines • EMC 860

Name _____

More Work and Less Work

This is a job that requires work.

If the job changes.

More Work

paste

Less Work

paste

This is a job that requires work.

If the job changes.

More Work

paste

Less Work

paste

 Simple Machines • EMC 860

Machines make work easier.

Abner's Story

Make transparencies of pages 23 and 24. As you read the story text below, cover all but the picture being described.

When you have finished telling the story have your students identify the machines that Abner used (clippers, rake, wheelbarrow, mower, wagon, wheeled bin, ramp, bike) and talk about how the machines made Abner's work easier.

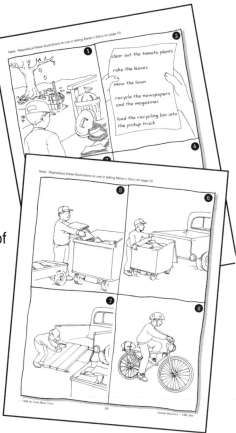

Picture 1 – Abner's mom told him that he had to clean up the backyard before he could go to the football game. Abner looked around at the mess that had collected over the last couple of weeks. This was a BIG job, but he really wanted to play football with his friends, so he would do his best.

Picture 2 – Abner read the list his mom gave him:
- clear out the tomato plants
- rake the leaves
- mow the lawn
- recycle the newspapers and the magazines
- load the recycling bin into the pickup truck

Picture 3 – Abner cut down the old tomato plants and threw them into the compost pit.

Picture 4 – He raked the leaves and mowed the lawn. He threw the grass clippings and the leaves into the pit.

Picture 5 – He loaded the stacks of newspapers and magazines into his wagon and pulled them over to the recycling bin.

Picture 6 – Abner pushed the bin over to the pickup. But he couldn't lift it up. How would he ever finish the jobs?

Picture 7 – Abner looked around and had a great idea. He made a ramp with four boards from his garage. Then he pushed the bin up the ramp and into the pickup's bed.

Picture 8 – Five minutes later Abner was on his way to the football game.

How to Make Work Easier

The three activities below may be conducted during a single or separate sessions. Record what happens and suggestions for making the work easier on a class logbook page entitled "How to Make Work Easier."

Cracking Nuts

Give students walnuts or almonds. Have them try to open the nuts using only their hands. Record what happens and ask for suggestions to make the work of cracking the nuts easier.

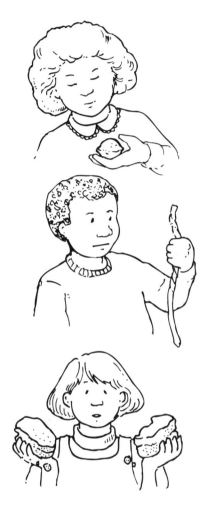

Stitching with Yarn

Give each student a length of yarn and a piece of burlap. Have them try to stitch a circle on the burlap using only their hands. Record what happens and ask for suggestions to make the work of stitching easier.

Cutting the Cake

Show the class two single unfrosted cake layers. Ask if they could divide the cake into equal pieces using their hands. Have someone try. Record what happens and ask for suggestions to make the work easier. (Students will probably suggest using a knife.) Have a student cut the other layer with a knife. Compare the pieces of cake cut by the knife to the ones torn by hand.

After conducting the activities, help students to draw the conclusion that machines or tools made the work easier. Ask students to tell other examples of work that is made easier by using machines. Record their responses on the class logbook page.

How to Make
Work Easier

I could not open the
nut with my hands.
We could use a nut
cracker or a
hammer to make it
easier.

Moving a Classmate

You will need a toy wagon and a large cardboard carton.

1. Have one student sit in the carton and another student sit in the bed of the wagon.
2. Ask students to predict which will be easier to push across the room.
3. Allow students to push the carton and then the wagon.
4. Help students to see that the wheels on the wagon made the work of moving the student easier.

They can generalize that machines make work easier.

Machines Make Work Easier

At School

Reproduce the logbook page on page 25. Students write and draw to tell how machines at school help them do work. Share the ideas with the class when the pages are completed.

At Home

Reproduce the individual logbook page on page 26. Students tell how machines used at home help to do work. Share the ideas with the class when the pages are returned to school.

Check for Understanding

Brainstorm ways that machines help do work.
List the ideas on a web that can become part of your class logbook.

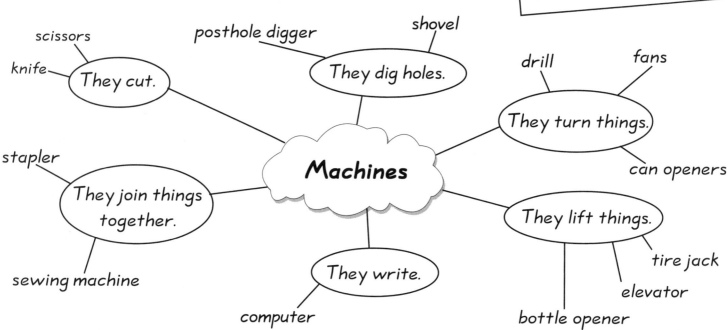

Note: Reproduce these illustrations to use in telling Abner's Story on page 20.

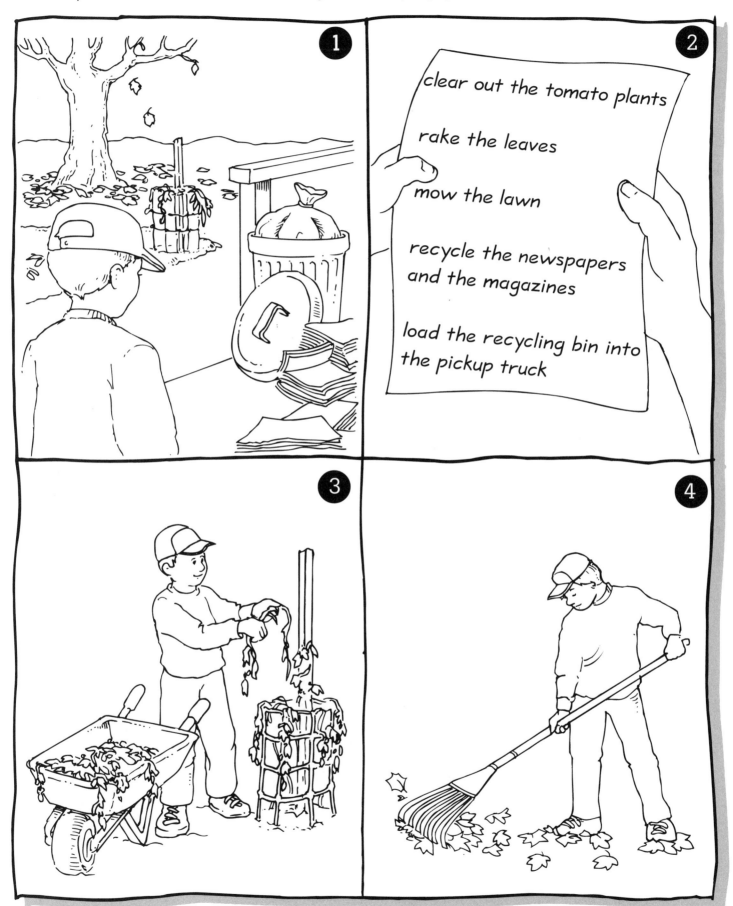

1

2

clear out the tomato plants

rake the leaves

mow the lawn

recycle the newspapers and the magazines

load the recycling bin into the pickup truck

3

4

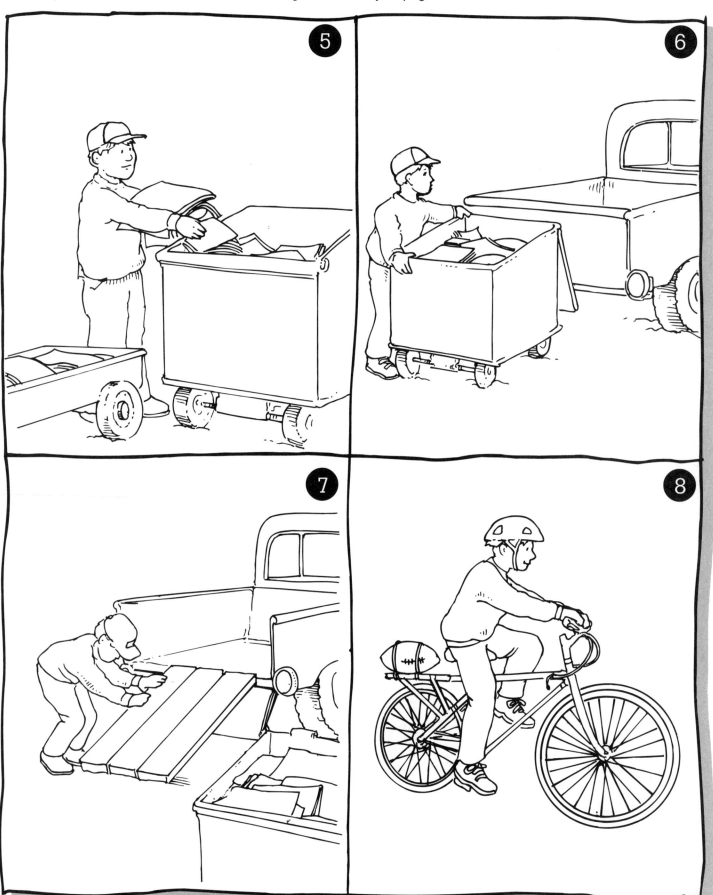

Name _____

Making Work Easier at School

Tell how you use each machine. Does it make your work easier?

_____

_____

_____

_____

_____

_____

_____

Draw another machine you use at school.

_____

_____

Name _____

Making Work Easier at Home

Machine	Do you have it?	Who uses it?	How does it make work easier?

Simple Machines • EMC 860

Machines may have few, many, or no moving parts.

Name the Tool

Prepare a display of tools and machines. Include things that are familiar to your students such as a hammer, an eggbeater, a pencil sharpener, a spoon, a curling iron, a toy car, a broom, a shovel, an electric drill, a bottle opener, etc.

Ask students to name each item and tell how it is used.

Begin a class logbook page entitled "Tools and Machines We Use."

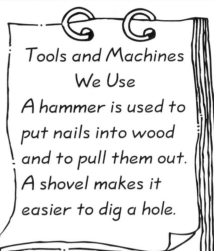

Tools and Machines
We Use
A hammer is used to
put nails into wood
and to pull them out.
A shovel makes it
easier to dig a hole.

Machines and Their Moving Parts

A Car

Make a transparency of the automobile on page 30.
Have students explain the work that an automobile does.
Ask students to describe the moving parts in the automobile.

It's always good to make connections with real things in your students' world. You may want to enlist a parent's help and use a real automobile to demonstrate some of the many moving parts. Park the car near your classroom and take a "field trip" to observe this complex machine. Some of the moving parts that you see will include the wheels, steering wheel, doors, windows, wipers, fan, gauges, belts, and handles.

A Can Opener

Show a hand-held can opener.
Have students explain the work that the can opener does.
Ask students to describe the moving parts of the can opener.

A Hammer

Show a hammer.
Have students explain the work that the hammer does.
Ask students to describe the moving parts of the hammer. *(The hammer has no moving parts.)*

Simple Machines • EMC 860

A Machine Center

- Set up a machine center in your classroom. Include the machines that you used to introduce this concept and add new ones from the lists below. Be sure to include those on the worksheet on page 31.

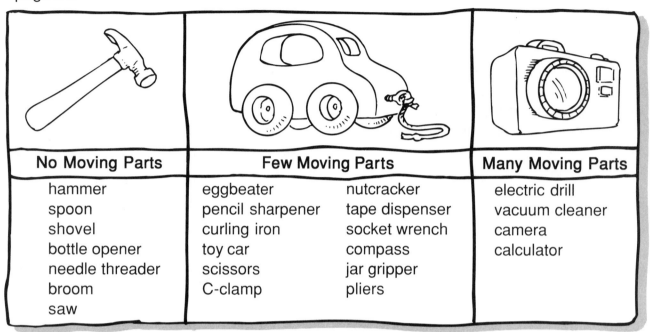

No Moving Parts	Few Moving Parts		Many Moving Parts
hammer	eggbeater	nutcracker	electric drill
spoon	pencil sharpener	tape dispenser	vacuum cleaner
shovel	curling iron	socket wrench	camera
bottle opener	toy car	compass	calculator
needle threader	scissors	jar gripper	
broom	C-clamp	pliers	
saw			

Confirm with students that each of the items in the center does work. Generate examples of the types of work that each machine does.

Allow each student time to investigate the machines and note their moving parts.

- Reproduce the activity sheet on page 31 for individual students and have students complete the sheet.

Classifying the Machines

After each student has had a chance to examine the machines in the center, sort the machines into groups:

    Machines with Many Moving Parts
    Machines with Few Moving Parts
    Machines with No Moving Parts

Record the groups on a chart for your class logbook. Confirm that all the machines do work, no matter which classification they fall into.

Simple Machines • EMC 860

Adopt-a-Machine Posters

- After their "Machine Center" discoveries, students will be ready to add additional machines to the class logbook list of "Tools and Machines We Use."

- Have each student choose a machine to "adopt" and make a poster for the adopted machine. Create a model poster similar to the one shown to share with the class before they begin their posters.

  Each poster should include:
  - a picture of the machine
  - the machine's name
  - an explanation of the work that the machine does
  - labels designating parts and noting whether they are moving parts

- Provide time for the students to present their machine posters to the class.

Worker Interviews

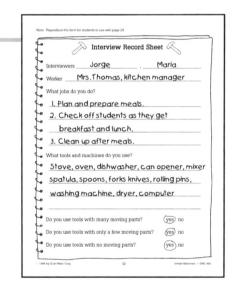

Assign pairs of students to interview school workers about the machines that help them work.

Reproduce the record sheet on page 32 and the note on the bottom of this page to provide school workers with the times and purpose of the interviews.

Have students role-play the questions that they will ask so that the interviews are productive.

After the interviews have pairs report to the class about some of the different machines that are used. Make sure to note which machines have many, a few, and no moving parts.

Dear Worker,

Our class is studying machines and how they help do work. This week we have been talking about how some machines have many moving parts, some machines have only a few moving parts, and some machines have no moving parts. We would like to talk to you about some of the machines you use to do your job.

Your interview is scheduled for_____

with _____ and _____.

Thank you for taking the time to meet with us.

Note: Make an overhead transparency of this form to use with page 27.

The Car

Simple Machines • EMC 860

Name _____

Machines and Their Moving Parts

Does each machine have moving parts? Mark **Yes** or **No**.
Then put an **X** on the moving parts that you discovered.

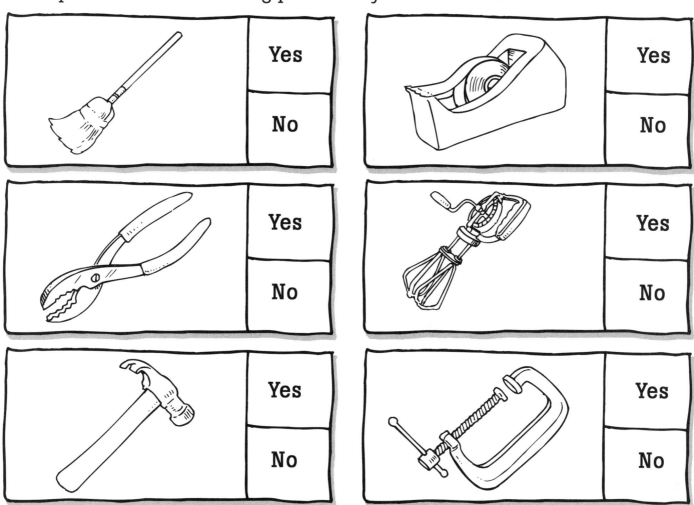

| | Yes |
| | No |

| | Yes |
| | No |

| | Yes |
| | No |

| | Yes |
| | No |

| | Yes |
| | No |

| | Yes |
| | No |

Draw a machine in each box. Mark any moving parts.

Simple Machines • EMC 860

Interview Record Sheet

Interviewers _____ , _____

Worker _____

What jobs do you do?

_____

_____

_____

_____

What tools and machines do you use?

_____

_____

_____

_____

Do you use tools with many moving parts?   yes   no

Do you use tools with only a few moving parts?   yes   no

Do you use tools with no moving parts?   yes   no

The Six Types of Simple Machines

Overview of pages 35-70

Each of the next six concepts focuses on one of the six simple machines, defining what it is and exploring its uses.

Students will work with each simple machine and then apply their observations to analyzing how all machines are made of one or more simple machines.

The chart below provides information for you about the six simple machines.

Lever

A lever is a bar used for raising or moving a weight. The weight is placed at one end and a force pushes down the other end. All levers have a turning point (fulcrum), a place where an object is moved, and an area where the force is applied.

A hammer and a crowbar are examples of levers that your students may have used.

Wheel and Axle

When a wheel is turned, the axle (a bar attached to the center of the wheel) turns, too.

Everyday machines that utilize a wheel and axle include the doorknob, the pencil sharpener, and the automobile.

Pulley

A pulley is a simple machine with one or more grooved wheels connected by a rope. A pulley makes it easier to move objects up, down, and across a long distance. The more pulleys you combine, the less force you need to move an object.

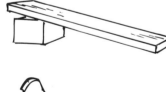

Inclined Plane

An inclined plane is a flat surface with one end raised higher than the other. It makes the work of moving things up and down easier.

Screw

The screw is a specialized inclined plane that is used to raise and lower things and also to hold things together. It is an inclined plane wrapped around a central pole.

Wedge

A wedge is also a type of inclined plane. It is wide at one end and tapers to a point at the other end. Wedges separate things by cutting, piercing, or splitting.

 Simple Machines • EMC 860

The Class Logbook

Create a page in your class logbook for each simple machine you explore. As you work with each machine, tell about the types of jobs it does and name some complex machines that include it. Use the open-ended logbook form on page 5 to record information for individual logbooks.

Picture Cards for Simple Machines

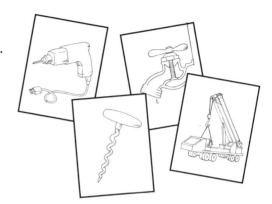

A page of picture cards is provided for each simple machine.
- Use the picture cards in your discussions of individual simple machines.
- Combine all the cards, have students draw a card, and identify the type of simple machine pictured.
- Combine the cards and have students sort them into groups according to type of simple machine.

Books with Simple Machines Projects

If you'd like to tackle projects beyond those in this unit, Gareth Stevens Publishing has some wonderful books:

Simple Science Projects series:
  Projects with Wheels by John Williams, 1987.
  Projects with Machines by John Williams, 1987.
Toy Box Science series:
  Levers by Chris Ollerenshaw and Pat Triggs, 1994.
  Gears by Chris Ollerenshaw and Pat Triggs, 1994.

Teacher Reference

For an understandable and entertaining explanation of simple machines (and more) read parts of *The Way Things Work* by David Macaulay, Houghton Mifflin, 1988.

The lever is a simple machine.

A Lever Makes Lifting Easier

1. Bring a long stick or narrow piece of wood and a cement block to your classroom.
2. Show how a lever works by having a student lift the cement block with the stick. Have the same student try to lift the cement block without the stick. Ask which was easier. (The lever makes the lifting easier.)
3. Let other students lift the cement block.

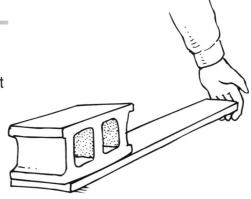

A Ruler as a Lever

1. Have students lift a heavy book with their hands.
2. Next lift the same book with a ruler.
   • Place a ruler across a small block to make a lever. The ruler should rest across the small block close to one end.
   • Place the book on the end of the ruler nearest the small block.
   • Press down gently on the other end of the ruler.
3. Ask students to compare the amount of work they did lifting the book with their hands and lifting the book with the lever.

You may choose to point out that the small block represents the **turning point** (fulcrum) of the lever. (The turning point is the place where the downward push changes into an upward force.)

Build a Model Seesaw

If possible, before building the model, observe the working of a real seesaw. Demonstrate how pushing down on one end of a seesaw causes the other end to move up.

Have students locate the turning point of the seesaw. Be sure to note that the seesaw makes the work of lifting easier.

Materials

- cardboard tubes cut in half the long way (1/2 tube per student)
- ruler (1 per student)
- bear counters (3 per student)
- "This Is How a Seesaw Works" form on page 40, reproduced for each student

Steps to Follow

1. Place the paper tube flat side down.
2. Balance a ruler across the tube.
3. Put a counter on one end. Tell what happens by drawing the seesaw on the record sheet.
4. Put a counter on the other end. Record what happens by drawing on the record sheet.

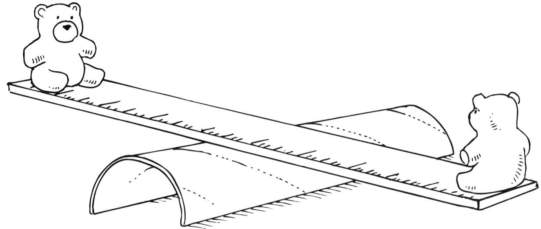

Follow Up

- When everyone has used their model seesaw, guide a discussion to explain their observations with questions like:

  "What happened when you put a counter on one end of the seesaw?"
  "What happened when you put a counter on each end?"
  "Where is the turning point of the seesaw lever?"

- Then challenge students to balance two counters on one side of the lever and one counter on the other. Have students draw to record their success on the record sheet. Share the various ways of solving this challenge. (Either shorten the side with the two counters or move the two counters closer to the turning point.)

- Students write their own challenges on file cards. For example: "Can you balance two counters on one side and four counters on the other side?"

  Put the challenge cards in a seesaw center with some model seesaws. When students working in the center solve the challenge, they should record the solution on the back of the card.

Using Levers for Jobs

Removing a Lid with a Lever

Bring in a metal container with a lid that must be pried up to open (such as oatmeal or tea tins, or home-repair products such as spackle). Make sure they are nontoxic.

1. Have students try to remove the can lid using their bare hands.
2. Then use a screwdriver as a lever to do the same job.
3. Guide a discussion of what happened with questions like these:

    "Is it possible to open the can with just your hands?"

    "Did the level make the work easier?"

    "How did it work?"

    "Where was the turning point?"

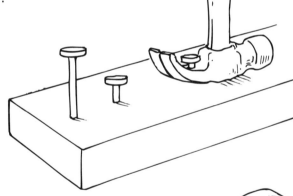

> A force was applied to one end of the lever; the other end lifted the lid up. The turning point was the edge of the paint can.

Pull Out a Nail with a Lever

Bring in a piece of wood with several large nails hammered partway in.

1. Have students try to remove a nail from a piece of wood with their hands.
2. Then use a hammer to pull out the nail.
3. Guide the discussion of what happened with questions like these:

    "Were you able to remove the nail with your hands?"

    "Was it hard?"

    "Did the hammer make the work easier?"

    "How did it work?"

    "Where was the turning point?"

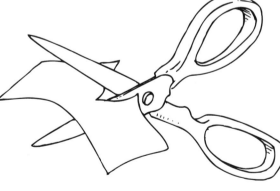

> The force was applied to the end of the hammer's handle, the metal teeth on the head of the hammer lifted the nail up. The turning point was where the head of the hammer rested on the board.

Cutting a Piece of Paper with Two Levers

If your students seem to understand levers, challenge them with this variation.

Tell students that a pair of scissors is two levers that have been combined. Cut a piece of paper to demonstrate the movement of the levers.

Have students tell what happened.

> When you open and close the scissors you can see the up and down movement of each of the levers. The turning point is in the center of the levers at the screw or rivet. The scissors also use a wedge on the edge of the blade to cut the paper more easily.

Summary Activities

- Reproduce the logbook form on page 41 to assess students' understanding of levers.

  Share the pages to make sure that students do not have any misconceptions about this simple machine.

- Take time to summarize your observations about levers in your class logbook and in individual logbooks if you wish. The entry might include ideas like these:

  A lever is a stiff bar that moves on a turning point. The bar can be straight or curved. Levers help us to move things by pushing, pulling, or lifting. When you use a crowbar or a screwdriver to pry something open, you are using a lever.

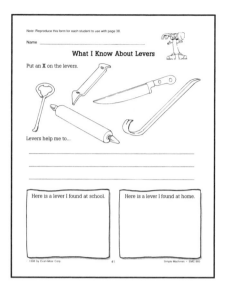

Note: Reproduce these picture cards to use when you are studying levers and to decorate your lever station during the "Machine Celebration" on page 74.

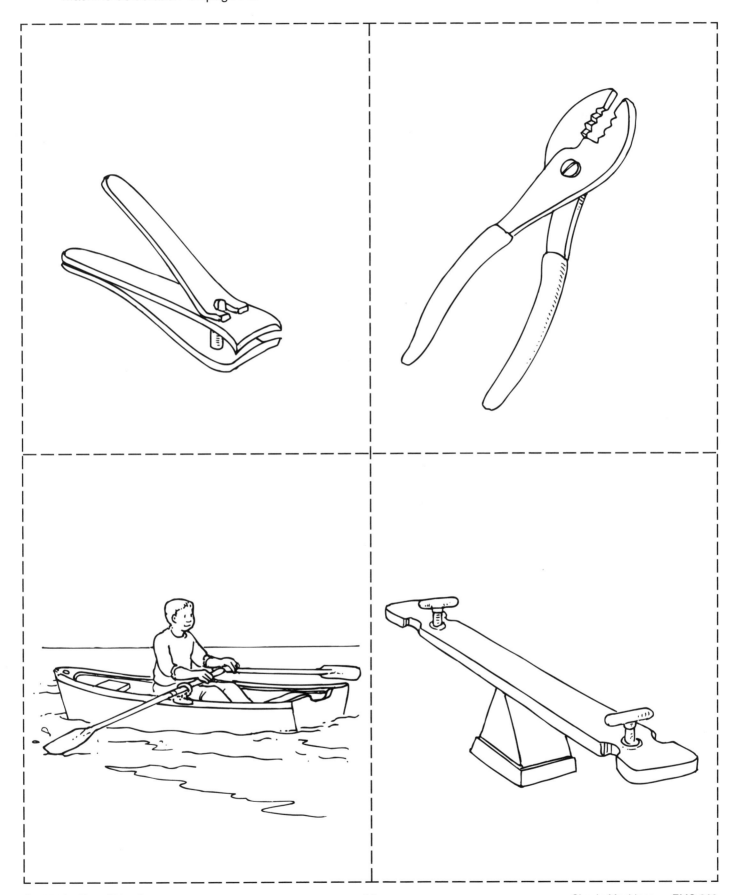

Name _____

This Is How a Seesaw Works

Draw the ruler with a counter on one end. Put an **X** on the turning point.

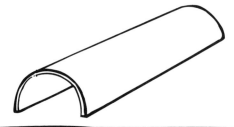

Draw the ruler balanced with a counter on each end. Put an **X** on the turning point.

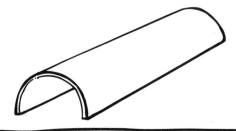

Challenge:
Draw the ruler balanced with two counters on one end and one counter on the other end. Put an **X** on the turning point.

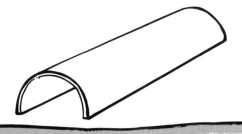

Note: Reproduce this form for each student to use with page 38.

Name _____

What I Know About Levers

Put an **X** on the levers.

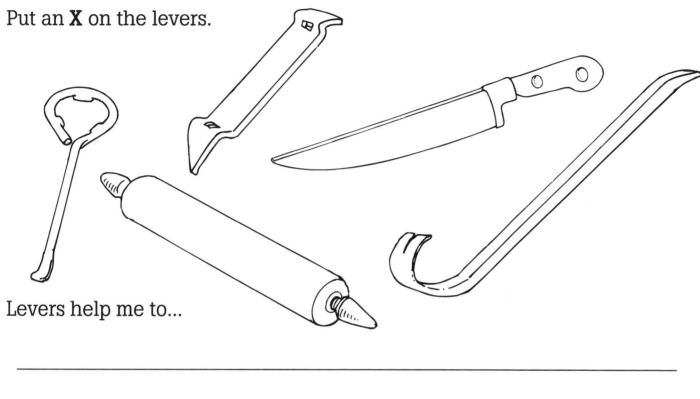

Levers help me to...

_____

_____

_____

Here is a lever I found at school.	Here is a lever I found at home.

Simple Machines • EMC 860

CONCEPT
The wheel and axle is a simple machine.

Examine a Doorknob

The doorknob is an everyday example of a wheel and axle. Bring in a doorknob or make a transparency of the doorknob on page 47.

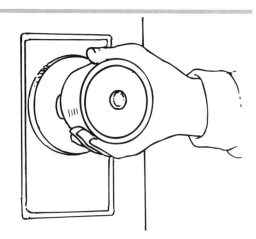

Identify the wheel and axle in the doorknob.
> The knob that you turn is the wheel.
> The inner rod that is attached to the knob is the axle.

Demonstrate how the wheel and axle works.
> Turning the knob (wheel) turns the inner rod (axle) and moves the latch. That movement opens the door.

A Wagon Uses Wheels and Axles

In an earlier lesson, your students used a wagon to show that machines make work easier. Take the time to analyze the wheel-and-axle portion of the wagon.

Turn the wagon upside down so that the wheels and axles are on top. Turn one wheel by hand and see what happens to the other wheel.

Point out the similarity and difference between the wagon and the doorknob. The wagon has a wheel at either end of a long axle. The doorknob has a wheel at either end of a short axle.

A Rolling Pin Station

Set up a station with Playdough® and a rolling pin. Let students practice flattening the dough with the pin.

Guide them to express these understandings:
> The rolling pin is a wheel and axle.
> When you push on the handles (the axle) the wheel turns and flattens out the dough.

Challenge students to think of other common machines that have one wheel like the rolling pin (wheelbarrow, top, and playground merry-go-round).

A Wheel and Axle Can Do Work

A winch is a type of machine that uses a wheel and axle to lift or pull something. One example of a winch is the old-fashioned wishing well where a wheel (the handle) is turned, causing the shaft (the axle) to rotate, raising or lowering a bucket. Winches can be seen at work on tow trucks, fishing reels, and hose reels.

Let small groups of students make a winch to demonstrate the lifting power of a wheel and axle.

Materials

- 2 ft (60 cm) length of 3/4" or 1" (2–2.5 cm) diameter PVC pipe
- two 6" (15 cm) pieces of 3/4" or 1" (2–2.5 cm) diameter PVC pipe
- 3/4" or 1" (2–2.5 cm) diameter PVC "T" joint
- 3 ft (90 cm) length of rope (school jump ropes would work)
- a small bucket such as a beach pail
- sand

Making the Winch

1. Slip the "T" joint on one end of the long piece of pipe.
2. Slip the 2 short pipe pieces onto the "T" joint, creating a handle.
3. Put the pipe between the tops of two chairs or two tables for support.
4. Tightly tie one end of the rope to the center of the pipe. You may want to secure it further with duct tape so that it doesn't slip.

Using the Winch

1. Fill the bucket half full with sand. Try lifting the bucket by hand.
2. Attach the bucket to the free end of the rope.
3. Turn the crank (wheel) to lift the bucket up to the pipe. Is it easier or harder to lift this time?
4. Add more sand. What happens to the force needed to turn the crank as more weight is added?
5. Record the experience by using the individual logbook form on page 5.

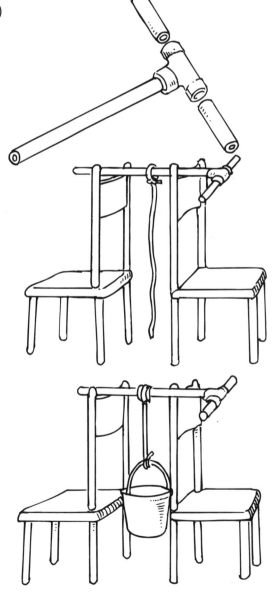

Special Wheels Called Gears

Defining Gears

Gears are inside nearly every machine that turns. Bring in several items with visible gears — a model clock, an eggbeater, a bicycle, a hand-operated can opener.

Show each item and demonstrate how the gears move. Ask your students to find a wheel and axle in each item. Tell students:
  "Gears are special wheels with teeth."
  "The teeth on the gears turn other gears."

Give students the opportunity to talk about other machines with gears that they have seen.

A Gear Center

Students will gain important information by exploring the way that the teeth move together and turn. Propose challenges and questions. Have students explore to solve them and then discuss their solutions.

  • Can you turn one gear and make another turn?
  • Can you turn one gear and make more than one other gear turn?
  • How many gears can you use in one system?
  • What happens when a small gear turns a larger gear?
  • What happens when a larger gear turns a smaller gear?

Purchase sets of plastic toy gears to use in the Gear Center or follow the instructions below to make your gears from Styrofoam® plates.

Make Gears from Picnic Plates

Materials

  • 2 or more Styrofoam® plates
  • scissors
  • long pins or nails
  • black marker

Steps to Follow

1. With the black marker, divide each plate into sixteen equal wedges. (For younger students, this step will need to be done in advance.)
2. Cut along each dividing line from the edge of the plate to the inside of the plate rim.
3. Trim off every other flap.
4. Round the corners of the teeth.

44

Summary Activities

- Take your students on a wheel and axle hunt around your classroom, through the school, and outside to the playground.

  When you return to the classroom, ask students to list some of the wheels and axles that they saw and record these on a class logbook page.

> A wheel turned on its side with the axle extending vertically is the basis for a number of different machines. The potter's wheel is a good example.

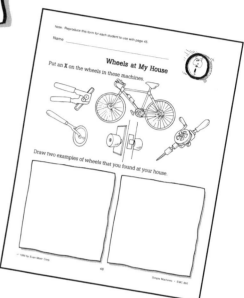

- Reproduce the record sheet on page 48 for individual students. Send the sheet home with them and have them find wheels and axles at their homes.

  Add the new items to your class logbook when the pages are returned.

- Challenge students to write and draw to show what their world would be like if there were no wheels. Share their observations and summarize the ideas for a class logbook page entitled "Without Wheels."

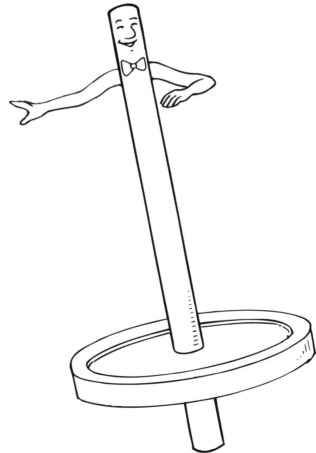

Note: Reproduce these picture cards to use when you are studying wheels and axles and to decorate your wheel and axle station during the "Machine Celebration" on page 74.

Simple Machines • EMC 860

A Doorknob Is a Wheel and Axle

Name _____

Wheels at My House

Put an **X** on the wheels in these machines.

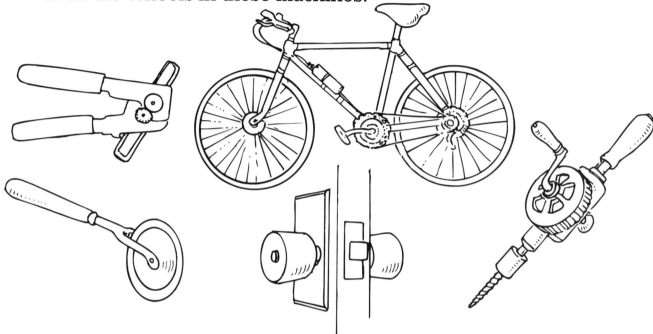

Draw two examples of wheels that you found at your house.

Simple Machines • EMC 860

The pulley is a simple machine.

The Flagpole

Enlist your custodian's assistance with this activity at your school flagpole.

Ask the students to suggest ways to get the flag on the top of the pole without moving their feet off the ground—the easiest way is to use a pulley attached to the top of the pole with a rope looped over it.

Demonstrate that when you pull down on one end of the rope, the pulley changes your downward pull into an upward pull and lifts the flag to the top of the pole.

A Pulley Center

Materials

• an eyehook screwed into a board at least a foot long. You will place the board between two tables, boxes, etc., where there is room to hang the pulley.
• 4 simple pulleys, 2 double pulleys — made following the directions below.
• a small container with a handle to hold the load (put a wire handle on a yogurt container)
• sand and/or small objects for the load
• heavy string
• task cards on pages 52 and 53

How to Make Your Own Pulleys

Materials

• pliable wire about the weight of that used in coat hangers
• wooden thread spools
• pliers
• wire cutters

A Simple Pulley

1. Push a piece of wire through the spool.
2. Use pliers to bend and twist the wire into the shape shown.
3. Cut the excess wire with the wire cutters.

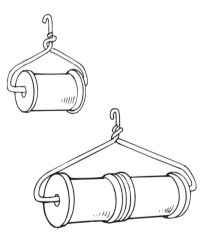

A Twin Pulley Block

1. Push a piece of wire through two spools positioned side by side.
2. Use the pliers to bend and twist the wire into the shape shown.
3. Cut the excess wire with the wire cutters.

Simple Machines • EMC 860

Using the Center

Have students explore using the pulleys alone and in combinations. The task cards challenge students to compare the amount of weight that can be lifted and the work that is done.

Record the results of student explorations on a class logbook page entitled "Pulley Power." Share their findings and check for understanding. If students have misconceptions, correct them at this point.

Answer Key for Tasks

Task 1–When you pull down, the load goes up, so the pulley changes the direction of the force. With a single pulley you cannot lift anything heavier than you could using just the strength of your arms.

Task 2–The double pulley system requires less force than the single pulley. The pulley makes the work easier and two pulleys make it two times easier.

Task 3–The quadruple pulley system makes lifting the load easier. Students should recognize the fact that each time you add a pulley to the system, the amount of work needed to lift the load is reduced.

Task 4–Students' drawings will vary depending on the number of pulleys that they used in their systems. Each time the string loops over or under a pulley, the direction of the force is changed.

Show Your Power

Demonstrate the power of pulleys with two broom handles and a rope.

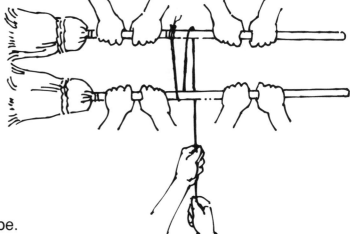

1. Ask four students to hold two broom handles apart.
2. Attach a length of rope to one handle and thread it around the other handle and back again as shown.

   Do your students recognize this threading pattern? *(It is the same pattern they used on the double pulley system. The broomsticks are acting as the spools.)*

3. Have a fifth student take the free end of the rope.
4. Explain that the fifth student will pull the rope to try to bring the broom handles together as the other four students try to hold their ground and keep the broom handles apart.
5. Have students predict what they think will happen.
6. Give the signal and have the fifth student pull.

The broom handles will come together easily. Why does this happen?
Is the fifth student stronger than the other four students together?

Remember, machines can make work easier. Which student is using a simple machine? *(The fifth student is using a pulley.)*

Summary Activities

Pulleys All Around

• Look for examples of pulleys in the real world.

Your school gym is a good place to start. Check the system that raises and lowers the basketball backboard. Are your climbing ropes lifted using a pulley?

The local garage may have a special pulley block to lift an engine out of a car to repair it. The mechanic wouldn't be able to lift the heavy engine without the pulley.

A ski lift uses a pulley to move a cable that helps to move people over and up mountains.

A farmer lifts a bale of hay up to a barn loft using a pulley.

Exercise machines use pulleys with weights attached to help people strengthen their muscles.

Sailors use pulleys to raise their sails.

A dragline uses pulleys to control its bucket and lift soil from the ground.

• If you're ambitious, videotape pulleys in use around the community. Talk with upper-grade teachers to see if any of their students are looking for a multimedia project.

• Have students draw or cut out pictures of machines with pulleys for a pulley collage. Mount the pictures along with student comments on a class logbook page. Then hoist the finished collage high in the room using a pulley.

Use Logbooks

• List the pulleys you have observed on the chalkboard. As a class, choose one pulley that you have observed.

As students describe the pulley to you, draw a diagram in your class logbook.

• Have individual students choose a different pulley to write about and draw in their individual logbooks. Read the pages to make sure that students do not have any misconceptions about this simple machine.

Pulleys All Around Us

Pulley Task 1
A Single Pulley

Loop the string over the pulley and
attach a load to one end.
Pull on the free end of the string.

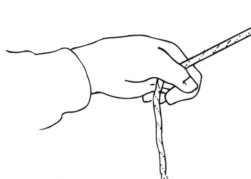

What happens?
Is it easier to lift the load with your arm or the pulley?

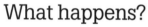

Pulley Task 2
A Double Pulley System

Use two simple pulleys.
Tie one end of the string to the top of the first pulley.
Loop the string under the lower pulley and then
back up over the top of the upper pulley.
Attach the load to the lower pulley.
Pull on the free end of the string.

What happens?
Was it easier to lift the load using one pulley or two?
Why do you think this is true?

Pulley Task 3
A Quadruple Pulley System

Use two twin pulley blocks.
Tie the string to the top hanger.
Loop it down under one of the lower pulleys,
up to the first pulley on the top hanger, back
down to the second lower pulley, and finally
back up to the second top pulley.
Attach the load to the lower twin pulley.
Pull the free end of the string.

What happens?
Does this quadruple pulley system make lifting the load
easier than the double pulley and the single pulley?
Tell why you think this happens.

Pulley Task 4
Set Up a System of Your Own

Use simple pulleys, a string, and a load.
Set up a new system that reduces the
force needed to lift the load.

Draw your system on a piece of paper.
Label the drawing to show where the force changes direction.

Simple Machines • EMC 860

Note: Reproduce these picture cards to use when you are studying pulleys and to decorate your pulley station during the "Machine Celebration" on page 74.

Simple Machines • EMC 860

CONCEPT
The inclined plane is a simple machine.

Using an Inclined Plane Makes Work Easier

• Recall how Abner cleaned up his backyard. Remind students that he used a ramp to load the trash cans into the pickup truck. A ramp makes moving heavy things easier. Ramps are examples of inclined planes.

Create an inclined plane in your classroom.
1. Rest one end of a wooden plank on the edge of a chair or a low table. Leave the other end on the floor.
2. Tie a heavy, wheeled toy such as a roller skate or a toy truck to a loop of string.
3. Have a student put a finger through the loop in the string and try to lift the toy the height of the top of the ramp.
4. Then have a different student put a finger through the loop and try to pull the toy up the inclined plane.
5. Give all students a chance to try the same demonstration.

• Reproduce the individual logbook form on page 58 so that each student can describe the experience of using an inclined plane.

An Inclined Plane Center

Set up a center where students can investigate inclined planes.

Stock your station with materials for making inclined planes and toys for trying out the planes once they are made.
    flat, heavy pieces of cardboard, long blocks, and wooden planks
    boxes or bricks
    wheeled toys
    string

Reproduce the challenge record sheet on page 59. Have students work in the center to solve the challenges and to create their own inclined plane system. They should record their solutions on the record sheet.

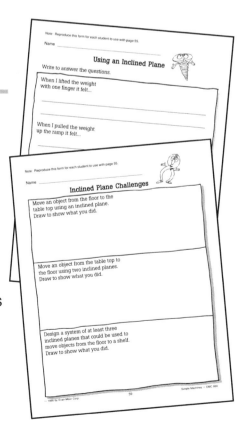

55   Simple Machines • EMC 860

A Special Inclined Plane

Explore a spiraling incline plane with this activity.

Steps to Follow

1. Reproduce the spiral pattern on page 60 for each student.
2. Have students cut out the spirals.
3. Tape the outside end of each spiral to a table or desk.
4. Pull the middle of the spiral up.
5. Ask students to describe what they see. Write some of their descriptions on a class logbook page entitled "A Special Inclined Plane."

Follow Up

Have students think of other spiraling inclined planes that they have seen — parking ramps in a large garage, circular staircases, and circular slides.

Discuss why this special kind of inclined plane might be used. *(It takes up less space than a straight ramp.)*

Summary Activities

Inclined Planes Around Me

• Walk around the school and the playground on a hunt for inclined planes. Each time one is spotted take time to discuss how it makes work easier. You might see:
>   a playground slide
>   a handicapped ramp
>   a loading ramp
>   conveyor belts
>   stairs (stairs are a special inclined plane with steps cut into them)

When you return to the classroom record your "finds" on a class logbook page entitled "Inclined Planes Around Us."

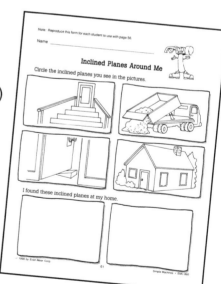

• Reproduce "Inclined Planes Around Me" on page 61 for students to complete as a home activity. Share responses when forms are returned and record any new inclined planes on the class logbook page.

Share Logbook Entries

Divide students into groups of three or four. Have them share what they wrote on the "Using an Inclined Plane" logbook form (page 58).

Make sure that students have no misconceptions about inclined planes.

Note: Reproduce these picture cards to use when you are studying inclined planes and to decorate your inclined plane station during the "Machine Celebration" on page 74.

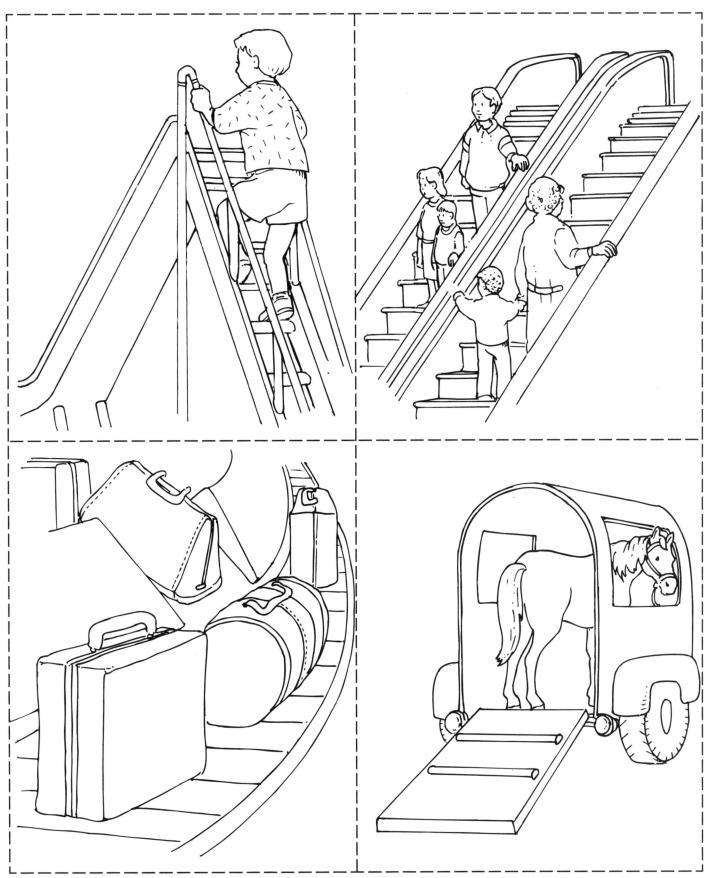

Note: Reproduce this form for each student to use with page 55.

Name ____

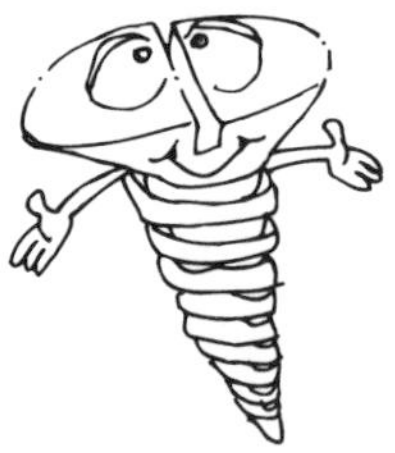

Using an Inclined Plane

Write to answer the questions.

When I lifted the weight
with one finger it felt...

____

____

When I pulled the weight
up the ramp it felt...

____

____

It was easier to...

____

____

Some Things to Think About

Did the height that the weight was moved change?	Yes	No
Did the distance that the weight had to move change?	Yes	No
Did the force that moved the weight change?	Yes	No

Name _____

Inclined Plane Challenges

Move an object from the floor to the
table top using an inclined plane.
Draw to show what you did.

Move an object from the table top to
the floor using two inclined planes.
Draw to show what you did.

Design a system of at least three
inclined planes that could be used to
move objects from the floor to a shelf.
Draw to show what you did.

       Simple Machines • EMC 860

Note: Reproduce this form for each student to use with page 56.

A Special Inclined Plane

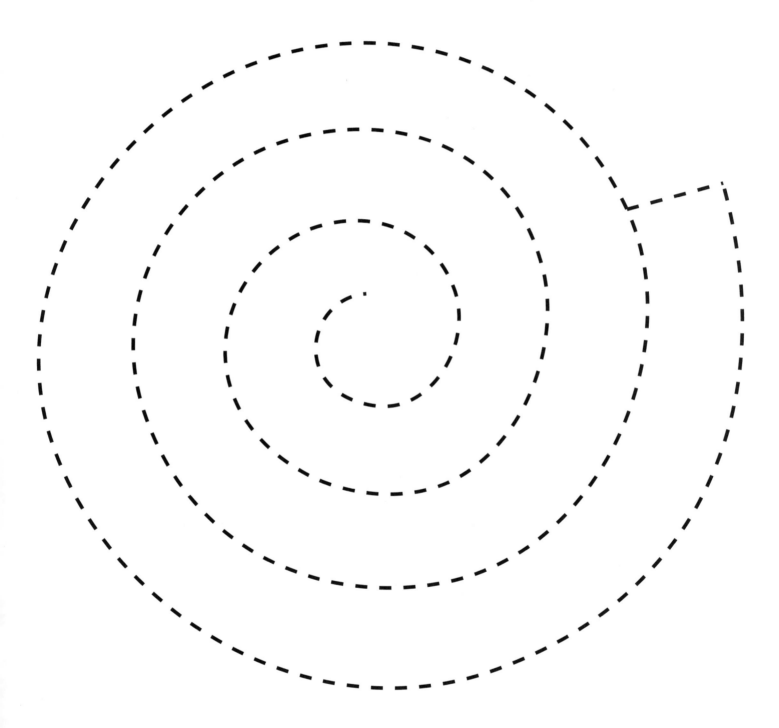

Simple Machines • EMC 860

Note: Reproduce this form for each student to use with page 56.

Name _____

Inclined Planes Around Me

Circle the inclined planes you see in the pictures.

I found these inclined planes at my home.

The screw is a simple machine.

What Is a Screw?

Help students to see that a screw is an inclined plane that curves around a central pole.

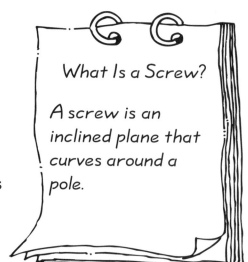

What Is a Screw?

A screw is an inclined plane that curves around a pole.

• Show the spiral inclined plane used in the activity on page 56. Review its name and how it helps do work.

• Show a real screw that is large enough for students to easily see the spiral thread. Make sure that students can name it as a screw. Ask them if they notice any similarity to the spiral inclined plane.

• Show actual tools that utilize a screw or use the picture cards on page 64. Have students point out the similarities among the different tools. Help them to recognize that all the tools have a screw part and that a screw is an inclined plane that curves around a pole.

• Record what was learned on a class logbook page entitled "What Is a Screw?"

Screws Help Move Things Up and Down

• Bring in a screw-type tire jack and demonstrate how it works. If possible have a parent volunteer show how the jack lifts the car.

Allow students to examine the jack closely. Have them locate the spiraling inclined plane.

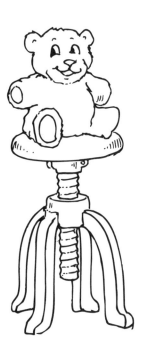

• A rotating stool is another example of a screw that moves things up and down.

Have a student sit on the seat. Turn the student around and watch as the seat moves up the screw mechanism, lifting the student.

• Record experiences on a class logbook page entitled "Screws Help Things Move Up and Down."

Screws Hold Things Together

- Demonstrate how a vise or C-clamp holds things together tightly. Point out the screw and show how it works.

- Sometimes a screw is put through two things to hold them together. Have students find examples of things in your classroom that are held together with screws. List the examples on a class logbook page entitled "Screws Hold Things Together."

- Reproduce the individual logbook form on page 65. Send the sheet home with students and have them record things in their homes that are held together with screws.

When the students return their logbook pages, share the experiences and add them to the class logbook.

Screws Hold Things Together

Screws hold the bulletin board to the wall.

There is a screw in my chair.

Summary Activity

This activity will allow you to check students' understanding of the screw.

Reproduce the tags on page 66. Give one to each student.

Have them find an example of a screw in the classroom or around the school. Then they will fill in the tag, describing the job that the screw does, and tie or tape it to the example. Check their work first to correct any misconceptions about this simple machine.

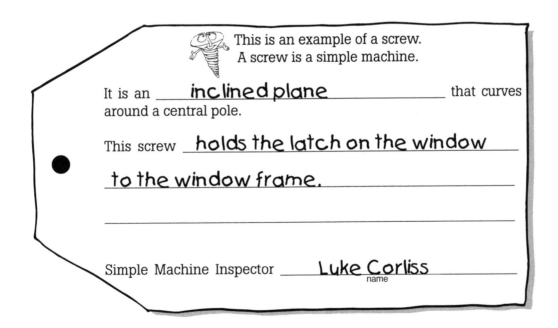

This is an example of a screw. A screw is a simple machine.

It is an _____inclined plane_____ that curves around a central pole.

This screw _____holds the latch on the window_____ _____to the window frame._____

Simple Machine Inspector _____Luke Corliss_____
name

Note: Reproduce these picture cards to use when you are studying screws and to decorate your screw station during the "Machine Celebration" on page 74.

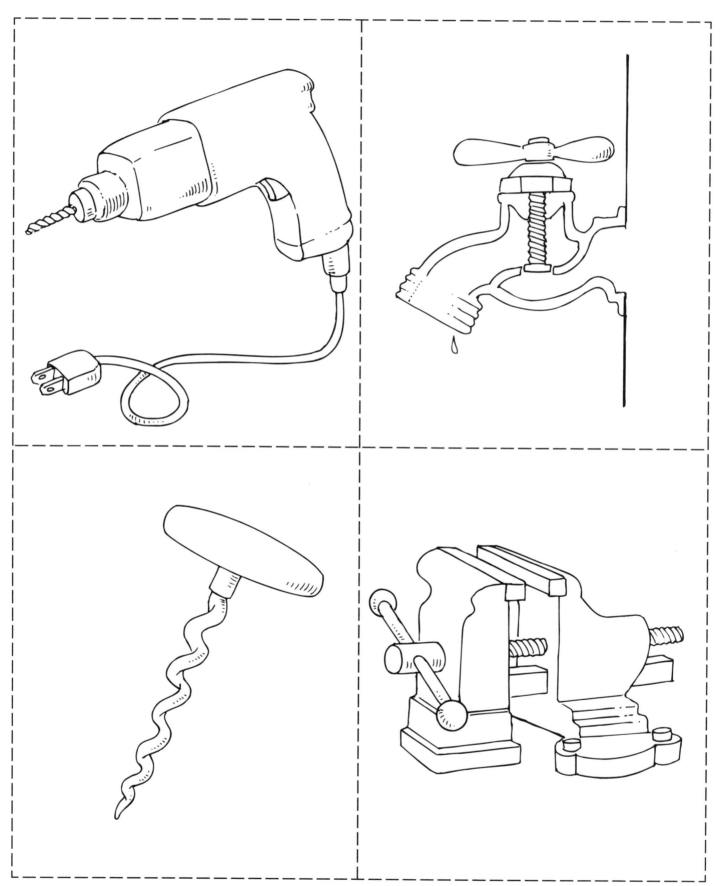

 Simple Machines • EMC 860

Name _____

Search for Screws

Draw to show four places that you found screws holding things together. Write to tell what is held together.

Note: Reproduce these tags for each student to use with page 63.

This is an example of a screw.
A screw is a simple machine.

It is an ______________________________ that curves around a central pole.

This screw ______________________________

____

____

Simple Machine Inspector ______________________________
name

This is an example of a screw.
A screw is a simple machine.

It is an ______________________________ that curves around a central pole.

This screw ______________________________

____

____

Simple Machine Inspector ______________________________
name

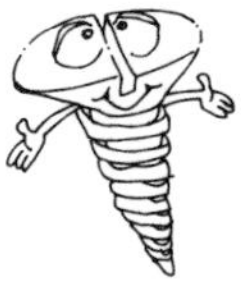

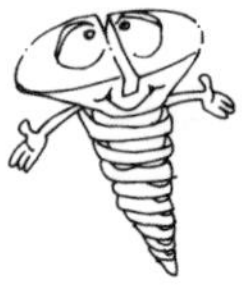

The wedge is a simple machine.

What Is a Wedge?

Help students to understand that a wedge is two inclined planes working together.

1. Show the class two right angle blocks. Guide them to recognize these as inclined planes.
2. Place the two blocks back to back. Explain that this double inclined plane is called a wedge.
3. Ask students to name things that have similar shapes. Show the picture cards on page 69 if more examples are needed.
4. Record the definition of a wedge on a class logbook page entitled "What Is a Wedge?" Add the examples named in the discussion.

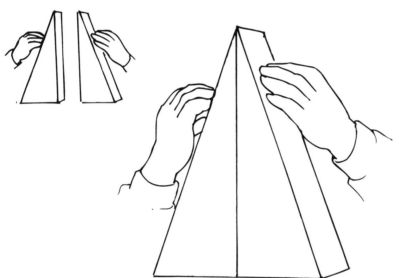

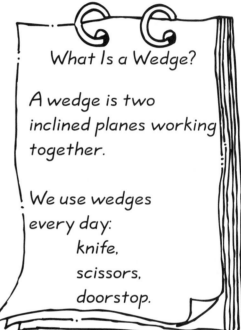

What Is a Wedge?

A wedge is two inclined planes working together.

We use wedges every day:
knife,
scissors,
doorstop.

What Do Wedges Do?

1. Bring a tool box to class. Fill the box with a variety of tools including a chisel, a knife, a screwdriver, nails, a saw, a hammer, a wrench, an ax, and a pair of pliers.
2. Look through the tool box with your students and identify the tools that are wedges (knife, chisel, screwdriver, nail, ax, and saw).
3. Discuss what jobs the wedge tools have in common. Help students to generalize that wedges separate things by cutting, piercing, or splitting.

Other Wedges Around Us

Many of the simple machines that we use daily are forms of the wedge.

• Show the following wedges and have students locate the double inclined plane and tell what the wedge does.

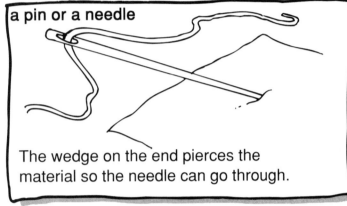

a pin or a needle

The wedge on the end pierces the material so the needle can go through.

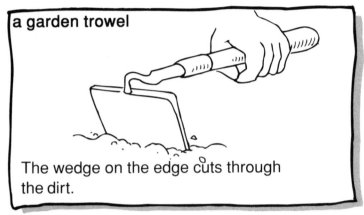

a garden trowel

The wedge on the edge cuts through the dirt.

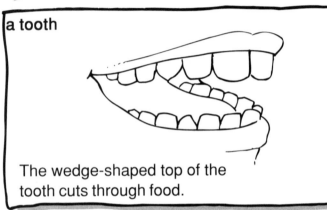

a tooth

The wedge-shaped top of the tooth cuts through food.

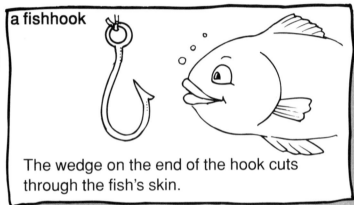

a fishhook

The wedge on the end of the hook cuts through the fish's skin.

• Reproduce the "Find the Wedges" activity sheet on page 70. Have students complete the page independently or in cooperative groups.

Summary Activity

During an individual conference or as an individual writing exercise, ask students to describe what a wedge does (pieces, splits, or cuts through). Have students draw or list several examples. Be sure to check responses to correct any misconceptions.

Note: Reproduce these picture cards to use when you are studying wedges and to decorate your wedge station during the "Machine Celebration" on page 74.

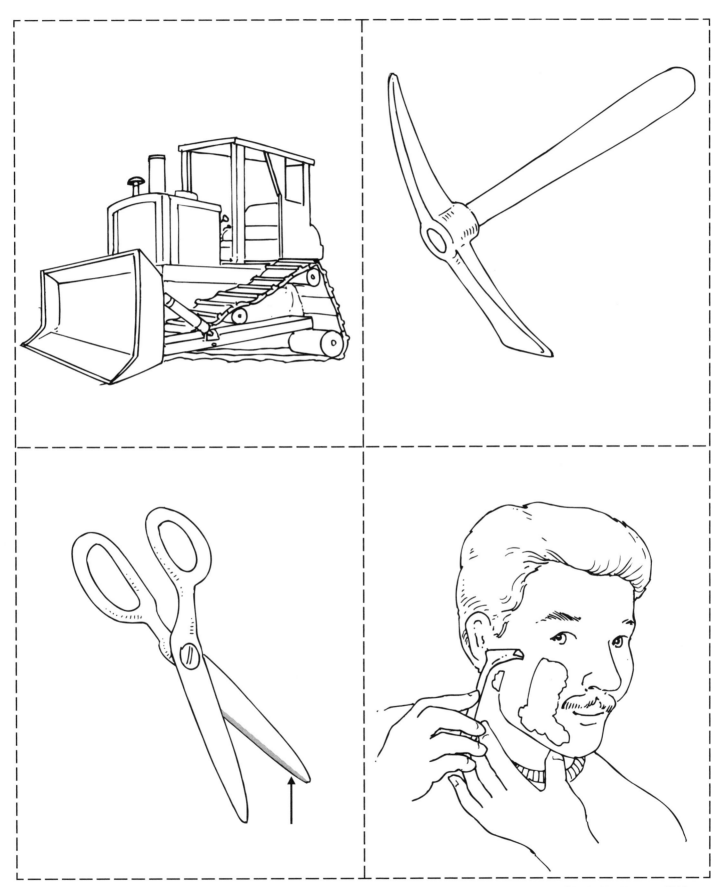

69

Name _____

Find the Wedges

Color the wedge on each tool.

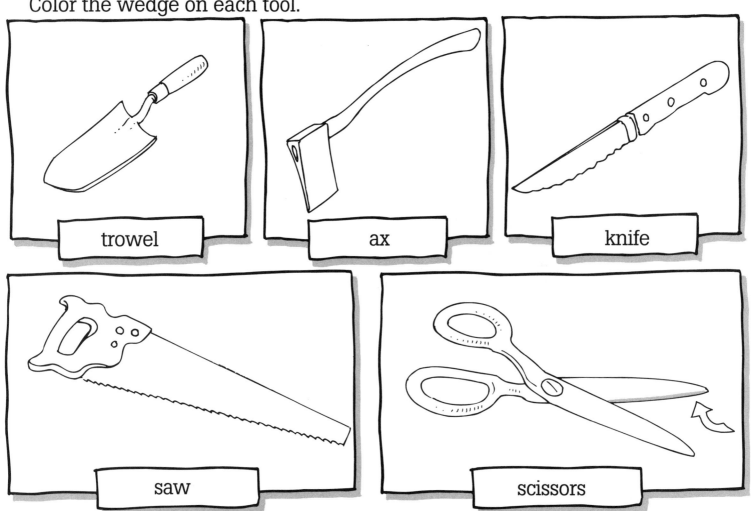

trowel

ax

knife

saw

scissors

Tell which wedge you would use to help you cut each thing.

an apple _____

a wooden plank_____

a pile of sand _____

a small tree _____

a piece of yarn_____

Simple Machines • EMC 860

All machines are made up of one or more simple machines.

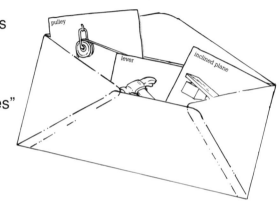

Analyzing Machines

In this exploration, groups of students will look closely at familiar machines and determine the simple machines that work together to help each machine do its work.

Getting Ready

• Reproduce 3 copies of page 73 for each group. Cut the cards apart and give each group a set in an envelope. Have some extra ones on hand.

• Make a large graph grid entitled "How many simple Machines" and label it as shown.

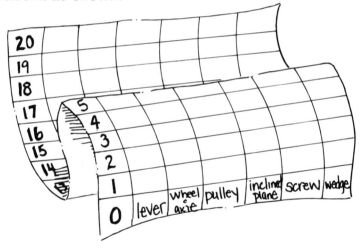

• Choose all or some of the machines shown below. You will need one machine for each small group of children. Depending on the number of groups, you may need to provide more than one of several machines. An analysis of each machine is provided to assist you.

• 2 levers
• wedge
• students may identify the rivet as a screw – clarify if you wish.

• 2 levers
• 2 wheels and axles
• wedge
• screw

• 1 lever
• 1 wedge

• 1 inclined plane
• 1 wedge
• 1 lever

• 1 wheel and axle
• 1 wedge

• 2 levers
• 2 wedges
• 1 screw

Simple Machines • EMC 860

Conducting the Activity

- Model the activity for students by analyzing an eggbeater.

"This eggbeater is made up of several simple machines. The handle I turn is a lever that is also part of a large wheel and axle. When the large wheel turns, it turns two smaller wheels and axles. The wheels have gears, too. The blades that do the work are wedges. So this machine has 1 lever, 3 wheels and axles, and 4 wedges." (Depending on the particular beater you have, there may also be one or more screws.)

- Form groups and give each group one machine and a set of simple machine picture cards. Familiarize students with the picture cards by holding up each card and asking its name.

  Ask each group in turn to hold up their machine and tell the class its name and what it is used for.

- Explain to the students that they are going to analyze their machines to see what simple machines they can find. Tell them that they will use the picture cards to show each simple machine they find.

- Guide students in an analysis of the machines, discussing one type of simple machine at a time. Instruct them to lay out a picture card for each example of that simple machine.

  "A lever is a bar that moves when force is applied to it. Examine your machine carefully. Do you see a lever? Do you see more than one lever? Talk in your group until you agree. Take a lever picture card for every lever you see in your machine."

Move around the groups to help with the analysis. Continue to guide the search for the other five simple machines.

Follow Up

- Present the "How Many Simple Machines?" graph grid.
- One group at a time, place the simple machine pictures in the correct column on the graph.
- Now take time to read your class graph. Ask students to explain the information that it reports. Prompt them with questions such as:

  "What simple machine is used most often in the machines in our classroom?"
  "What simple machine is used the least?"
  "How many more wedges than inclined planes are there?"

         Simple Machines • EMC 860

73

pulley

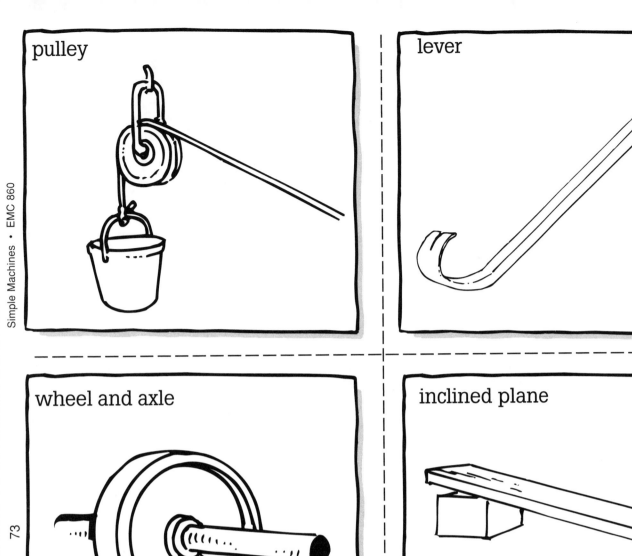

lever

wheel and axle

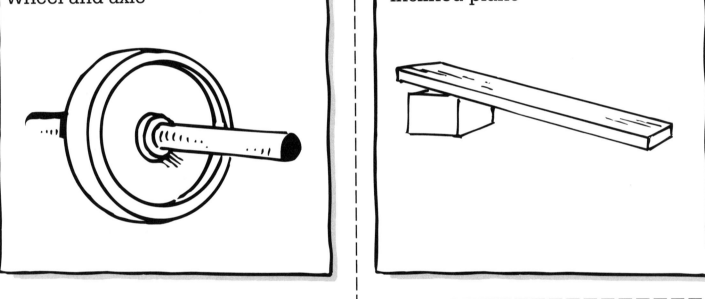

inclined plane

wedge

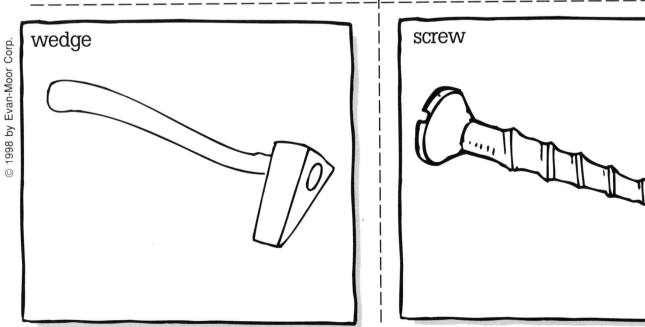

screw

A Machine Celebration

Celebrate your new understanding and appreciation for machines with a machine celebration.

Getting Ready

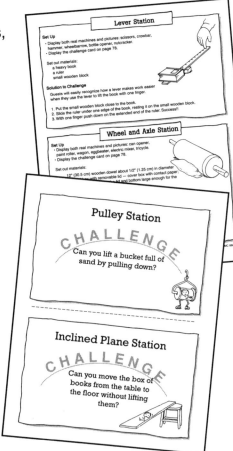

- Decorate the room with items from your machine studies — posters, graphs, and class logbook pages.

- Set up stations representing the six simple machines. Complete directions and signs for the six stations begin on page 75.

- Let students color and cut out badges for celebration guests. (See pattern on bottom of this page.)

- Choose pairs of students to man each station. Students should be prepared to answer questions about their simple machine. Every student needs to have a job, so assign other students to welcome and guide guests through the celebration.

- Invite parents or another class to your celebration.

- Prepare a snack to serve. Be sure to make a poster listing the machines that you used in preparing the snack.

- Display individual and class logbooks for your guests to read.

Lever Station

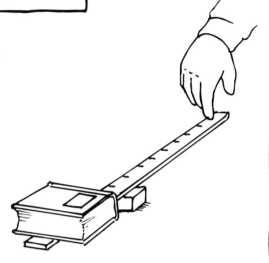

Set Up

- Display both real machines and pictures: scissors, crowbar, hammer, wheelbarrow, bottle opener, nutcracker.
- Display the challenge card on page 78.

Set out materials:
   a heavy book
   a ruler
   small wooden block

Solution to Challenge

Guests will easily recognize how a lever makes work easier when they use the lever to lift the book with one finger.

1. Put the small wooden block close to the book.
2. Slide the ruler under one edge of the book, resting it on the small wooden block.
3. With one finger push down on the extended end of the ruler. Success!!

Wheel and Axle Station

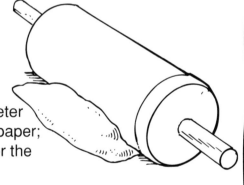

Set Up

- Display both real machines and pictures: can opener, paint roller, wagon, eggbeater, electric mixer, tricycle.
- Display the challenge card on page 78.

Set out materials:

   12" (30.5 cm) wooden dowel about 1/2" (1.25 cm) in diameter
   oatmeal box with removable lid — cover box with contact paper;
      make a hole in the lid and bottom large enough for the
      dowel to fit through
   bag of beans
   Playdough®

Solution to Challenge

Guests will make a rolling pin from the dowel and oatmeal box. They may discover that putting the beans into the box before putting the dowel through gives the roller more weight and flattens the dough more efficiently.

1. Put dowel through hole in the bottom of box and extend it out the open end.
2. Pour in beans.
3. Put lid onto dowel and slide down to close box.
4. Roll the box over the lump of Playdough® to flatten it. Success!!

Pulley Station

Set Up

• Display both real pulleys and pictures of pulleys.
• Display the challenge card on page 79.

Set out materials:
  a small pulley
  twine
  buckets made from yogurt cups with wire handles
  sand
  a place to hang the pulley

Solution to Challenge

Guests will loop the twine over the pulley and use pulley power to reverse the direction of the force. They will pull down to lift the bucket up.

1. Hang up the pulley.
2. Tie one end of the twine to the handle of the bucket.
3. Loop the free end of the twine over the pulley.
4. Pull down on the free end to lift the bucket. Success!!

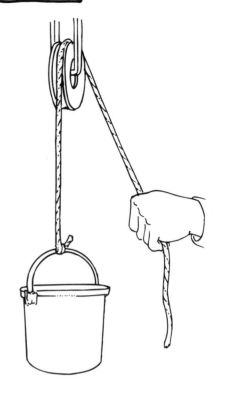

Inclined Plane Station

Set Up

• Display both real inclined planes and pictures of inclined planes: ramp, funnel, shoehorn, toy dump truck.
• Display the challenge card on page 79.

Set out materials:
  wooden planks of varying lengths
  box of books
  table
  chair

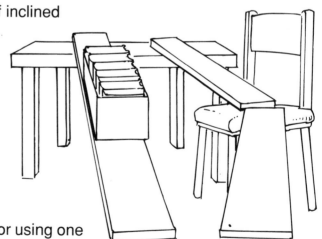

Solution to Challenge

Guests will create a ramp from the table to the floor using one wooden plank or a series of smaller ramps using shorter planks.

1. Make an inclined plane from the table to the floor using one or more wooden planks.
2. Push the box down the inclined plane. Success!!

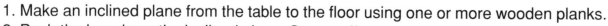

Screw Station

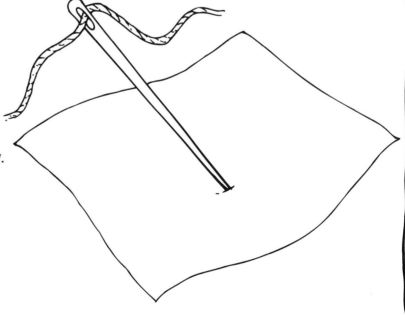

Set Up

- Display both real machines and pictures: corkscrew, jack, hand drill, assorted screws, crank pencil sharpener with cover removed.
- Display the challenge card on page 80.

Set out materials:
  several C-clamps
  6" (15 cm) square of plywood
  desk or table edge

Solution to Challenge

Guests will use the C-clamps to fasten the plywood to the desk.

1. Lay the plywood on the edge of the desk.
2. Put one edge of the C-clamp above the plywood and the other edge below the desk.
3. Twist the little handle to tighten the screw and fasten the two together.
4. Add another clamp for security. Success!!

Wedge Station

Set Up

- Display both real machines and pictures: doorstop, table knife, chisel, garden trowel, fishhook.
- Display the challenge card on page 80.

Set out materials:
  small squares of felt
  pieces of yarn
  needles with large eyes

Solution to Challenge

Guests will thread the needles and sew.

1. Thread the needle with the yarn.
2. Stitch across the felt. Success!!

Lever Station

CHALLENGE

Can you lift the book
with one finger?

Wheel and Axle Station

CHALLENGE

Can you flatten the
dough using a wheel
and axle?

Pulley Station

CHALLENGE

Can you lift a bucket full of sand by pulling down?

Inclined Plane Station

CHALLENGE

Can you move the box of books from the table to the floor without lifting them?

Screw Station

CHALLENGE

Can you fasten the
plywood to the desk?

Wedge Station

CHALLENGE

Can you sew a line
across the felt?